To Dan Venecek and Linda Zollo.
Ponds can be deep, like friendship.
DE

For Charlie and our five turtle days
AS

Text copyright © 2022 by David Elliott
Illustrations copyright © 2022 by Amy Schimler-Safford

First edition 2022

Library of Congress Catalog Card Number pending
ISBN 978-1-5362-0598-5

21 22 23 24 25 26 APS 10 9 8 7 6 5 4 3 2 1

Printed in Humen, Dongguan, China

This book was typeset in Columbus.
The illustrations were done in mixed media and finished digitally.

Candlewick Press
99 Dover Street
Somerville, Massachusetts 02144

www.candlewick.com

AT THE POND

David Elliott

illustrated by

Amy Schimler-Safford

CANDLEWICK PRESS

The red-winged blackbird spreads his tail
and sings his hello morning song;
he has sung it since the bright
and misty world began.
The bullfrog leaps!
And there among the reeds,
the water ripples like a fan
unfolding on the surface of the pond.
It springs to life! Another day has dawned.

What a swimming portrait
the dabbing mallards make:
the mottled hen, the ducklings,
and behind, the splendid drake.

The water lilies open
in the morning sun.
Frog sits on a lily pad:
the show has just begun.
She's come to watch
the lilies open
one
by one
by one.

His reputation swims well
beyond the banks of the pond.
The stories he has spawned
have been repeated so often
no one knows truth
from exaggeration.
They have even given him
a loving appellation: Old Harry,
the Catfish That Won't Be Caught.

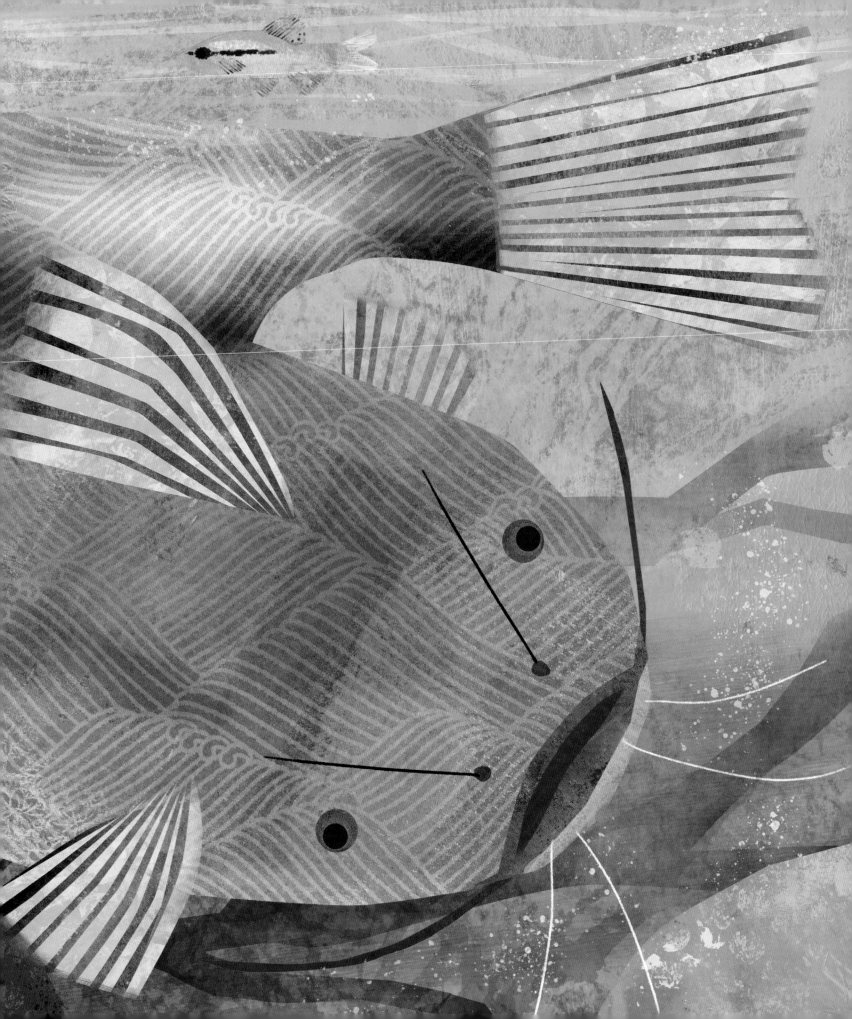

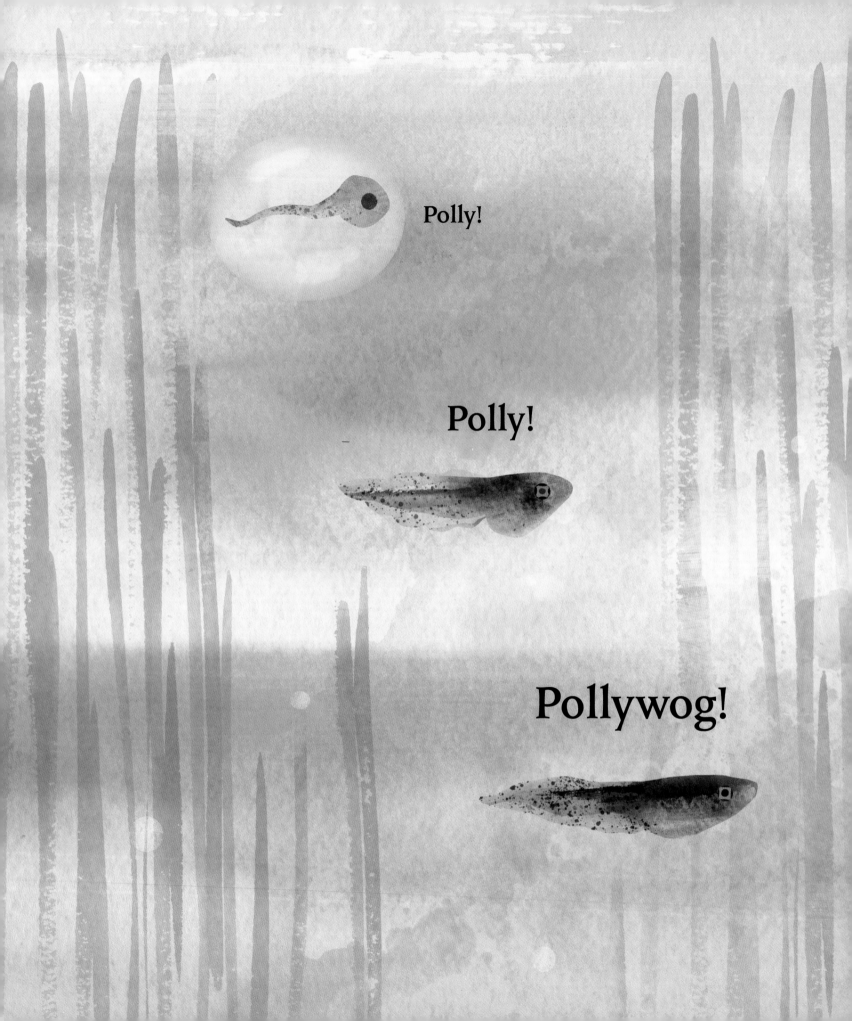

Polly!

Polly!

Pollywog!

At the bottom
of the pond the
hungry snapping
turtle waits, where
an unsuspecting
minnow will meet
its hard-shelled fate.

The dragonfly:
delicate,
diaphanous,
dazzling,

yet

fundamentally
ferocious
as fierce
as any fighter

jet.

The water strider:
enigmatic
but prolific.
Each day
he writes
his story
in rippling
hieroglyphics.

They shatter the burnished surface
into shards of splintered light.
The day is hot, the water cool.
What does it matter
that the turtles slide from their log
or the startled geese take flight?

To watch her from
some distance
is probably best.
The water snake
is guarding
her teeming,
knotted nest.

Rising from the pond—
a hodgepodge dome.
But inside the beaver's
stick-built home
it's as cozy as can be,
and the essence
of a beaver's thoughts
on domesticity.

The pond's nobility,
the great blue heron wades
in the shallows with ancestral dignity
~~both majestic~~ and absurd.
The fish do not doubt it:
the heron is a striking bird.

In the silvered evening's dim
the little muskrat comes to swim
over boulder, sunken limb.
The pond would be a different pond
without the busy, swimming him.

Now, the evening light is fading,
but there are other creatures waiting
to walk out from the shadows where they hide.
The deer, her fawn close by her side,
comes to the softly charcoaled shoreline first.
They bow their heads to satisfy their thirst
while the charismatic fireflies
blink their silent lullabies.
Soon, the fickle moon will pass
across the nighttime looking glass.

Cattails whisper through the night
until the morning's welcome light
finds the pond's expectant shore

and the blackbird sings

once more.

Notes About the Animals and Plants

RED-WINGED BLACKBIRDS: It doesn't seem quite fair that this popular songbird's name applies to just half its population. It's only the males that have those bright-red shoulders with the yellow stripes. The female is neither red-winged nor black, but a streaky dark brown.

MALLARDS: Mallards are the ancestors of almost all farmyard ducks. They're speedy, too, and have been clocked flying at a whopping 55 miles (88 kilometers) an hour. Want to sound smart? A flock of mallards is called a sord.

WATER LILIES: Water lilies are not just beautiful; they also play an important role in the health of a pond. Their showy flowers and pads work to shade the water. This helps keep the temperature down, which in turn slows the growth of algae.

CATFISH: Ever wonder what those whiskers on a catfish are actually called? Barbels. Barbels help catfish search for food in the murky water where they live. In the United States, catfish have a lot of nicknames: mud cats, chuckleheads, scoopers, and flatties.

POLLYWOGS: When we think about pollywogs, we almost always think about metamorphosis. That's the process in which an animal changes from one form into another, kind of like a shapeshifter that takes its time. In one of the last stages of a pollywog's metamorphosis, just before it becomes a frog, its mouth widens and its intestines become shorter. Ouch!

BULLFROGS: You wouldn't know it to look at them, but bullfrogs are amazing athletes. They can jump up to ten times their body length. Think about that. The average height of a nine-year-old American girl is 4 feet 4 inches. That's 52 inches (133 centimeters). If that girl were a frog, she would be able to jump 520 inches, or a little over 43 feet (13 meters). That's about as long as a sleeping brachiosaurus!

SNAPPING TURTLES: Unlike most other turtles, snapping turtles cannot pull their head and legs into their shell. This is because their plastron, the hard plate that covers their underside, is smaller than the plastrons of other turtles. Scientists think that this vulnerability is one of the reasons snapping turtles are so aggressive on land. In the water, they are rather docile and curious. They've even been known to give a swimmer's leg a friendly bump with their nose.

DRAGONFLIES: Most of us picture dragonflies hovering over the surface of a pond, their iridescent colors glinting in the sun. But a dragonfly spends its first two years underwater. Because dragonflies can fly up, down, sideways, and even backward, they are very efficient hunters. They also have super sharp teeth. Luckily, most dragonflies are not large enough to bite humans.

WATER STRIDERS: Like all insects, water striders have six legs. The short front pair grasp prey as the strider skates along the surface of the water. The middle pair function as paddles and the last pair as brakes. All six of those legs are covered with tiny hairs that trap bubbles, allowing the water strider to stay on the surface.

TURTLES/CANADA GEESE: When you see pond turtles basking on a log, they're soaking up the vitamin D that helps to harden their shells. And what do Canada geese have in common with a pet cat? They purr when they are content.

WATER SNAKES: Though they can be aggressive, water snakes are nonvenomous and therefore basically harmless. Unfortunately, they can be easily mistaken for the poisonous water moccasin. As with other wild creatures, if you see a snake, best to give it plenty of room.

BEAVERS: A beaver's lodge typically has two rooms: a smaller one at the lower level for eating, and a larger one, a little higher up, where the beavers raise their young. But who is living in that lodge? The mother and father beaver, their current litter, and maybe even last year's litter, too—all in all, anywhere from four to eighteen family members.

GREAT BLUE HERONS: Unlike your parents, a great blue heron never reminds its young to chew their food. Why? These birds swallow their food whole. Herons like to nest in colonies, called heronries. Some heronries have up to five hundred nests.

MUSKRATS: In spite of its name, the muskrat is not a rat, but is in fact more closely related to voles and lemmings. Muskrats can swim underwater for almost twenty minutes.

FIREFLIES: Imagine if you had organs in your stomach that lit up. Well, fireflies do. These beetles take in oxygen and mix it with a special substance called luciferin. The result is light. Scientists still aren't sure how fireflies turn that light on and off. Here's something strange: some adult fireflies do not eat.

CATTAILS: Most kids think cattails look like hot dogs. In fact, that long brown sausage shape is a collection of tiny female flowers. Not very tasty, I'm afraid. But part of the cattail is edible: more than 30,000 years ago, hunter-gatherers made flour from its rhizome, or root.